IN STORM & STILLWATER

In Storm & Stillwater

Ifunanya Georgia Ezeano

QUERENCIA

Querencia Press - Chicago, IL

QUERENCIA PRESS

© Copyright 2025
Ifunanya Georgia Ezeano

ISBN 978 1 963943 20 7

www.querenciapress.com

First Published in 2025

Querencia Press, LLC
Chicago IL

Printed & Bound in the United States of America

Men are the strongest when women fail to show their strength.

Dedicated to every poet,
dead or alive.

CONTENTS

IN
STORM

IF I EVER GO FOR A GROUP THERAPY

If I ever go for a group therapy, this is how I will introduce myself. My name is Georgia or Ifunanya, so long you don't mispronounce it.

I am a fixer, this means I'm naturally attracted to broken things. I don't have many problems—just Insomnia, PTSD, Imposter syndrome, childhood trauma, anxiety, micro passive aggression, a couple of health issues for beautification. I shrink in a group so I won't be noticed, but somehow garner attention for being quiet. Self-sabotage is how I show myself love. I apologized to the door knob that tore my best dress, but in my head I meant, *Fuck, Fuck, Fuck-shit.* My favorite song is silence, it helps cook my favourite dish—poetry. I live somewhere in the future next door to the past. The present is just my means of getting home. My outward look can be likened to the Zuma rock, on the inside, cotton candy, will be green-eyed. Love is a mystery to me. People mistake my kindness for love and I mistake their fondness for affection. The first day my father saw me, he thought I was a boy. He still chases after the man in me.

THE FORGOTTEN ART OF SEPPUKU: A MODERN RITE OF PASSAGE

Brown angels live in this rocky city
they are a body of water fitted into a room
their ears are magnets for garish waves
On their good days their feet are cold in fire
unwilling to hold up their mass
but ships sail across their abdomen
Their shores are filled with
fading laughter they cannot identify
with rooted loud cries that echo in notes
this stillwater does not eat up life
this ocean has washed strangers clean
and drowned its sons
They stir up waves and storm for comfort clenching moist
mouth, dusty teeth, and morally grey breasts holding treasures
buried in layers and layers of reluctant robes
Boys in this town dread flowers
but girls in this city grow flower conservatory
in land where their legs meet
When their dream turns into a nightmare
they fight their eyelids to unwrap
Night comes again but they're now aardvarks
Fluent in tongues that appall demons

ANGER MANAGEMENT MASTER CLASS

If you are a girl sitting at the entrance of a mall and your period cramps are eating you raw, then a man walks up to you saying: hey miss, smile! punch him in the face. If anyone is talking down on the womb that made you or talking about your father's job like he's not another hero without a cape, punch him in the face. This is the third time you're booked for fat reduction surgery but a stranger thinks obesity is another dry joke to crack, punch him in the face. In this class I'm not teaching you how not be angry, you are learning how to prolong your reaction. We are measured by our show of anger, like our kindness was not taken for granted. A boy cannot show emotions but is dreaded by the height of his rage, as if anger is not an emotion. Anger is a characteristic of a living thing but love is the way to grow its embers, raucous. A woman cannot express anger lest she risk being called bitter. Anger is a good emotion, it helps you say FUCK YOU when need be. It helps you leave the table when your ass is the meal. When an angry father moulds an angrier daughter a disaster is born. He teaches her how to throw punches in self-defense but the world encourages her to throw the first punch, tight your fist, and cry the loudest.

UNLIKE OTHER GOOD THINGS, GRIEF DOESN'T DECAY—IT LURKS.

It waits till you are dancing to your old favorite song, too give you a quick slide show in HD: a smiling face of your favourite uncle, images of him teaching you how to let yourself flow with the rhythm of this song he forced you to listen to, a bright projection of his body sliced into equal parts lying side by side on a heap of dirt in a busy Lagos road. Mom has ordered you to write your exams, she can sob for two. You remember you are not a soldier. You are just a wild child life is taming. It's has been 10 years but you still have tears to waste.

STURDY FAITH

What mountain can I not climb by faith?
As a child, I convinced death that I was worthy of living.
Every night, I pray for the world to be better,
But when I wake up,
Hurricane in the East,
Tsunami in the West.
What wind will blow me off my root?
The sea that tried to swallow me, threw me up.
Here I am.
I have stepped into earthquakes
and some earthquakes waddled toward me.

I survived.

FAR ACROSS THE ATLANTIC

Far across the Atlantic

in search of grass, greener

I ruminate

My fatherland is deep rooted in manure

yet the gardeners fail to water it.

I tried to weed my portion but they sent locust to eat my sprouting seed. Starved of choice, I left.

My brother stayed back, with courage and pain he eats what is left of the land. The gardeners let him sing their praises and gift him expensive rags.

On my way across the west Pacific ocean, it seemed agony still awaits me, but there, a little polished.

Today, anytime I eat, I wish my homeland gave me more.

But if I die in the shores of Sahara

Or be gunned down by a cop in Los Angeles,

wrap me up in a body bag, bring me back to my motherland, and place me horizontally on mother earth.

When the rain falls I promise to make farms greener so our children won't follow my path.

STAGES OF HEARTBREAK

One

Anger

Burns your heart at 2 am, perforates your belly tender and continuous.

Be careful not to say the thing you can't take back and thunder the things you have stomached for long. Unleash your unseen dragon calmly or not.

Two

Confusion

The cliché line "it's not you, it's me" chases you in your daydreams and gives you horrifying nightmares.

Was my kindness not commensurate to his ego? Should I apologize for being selfless? Was this really a thing? Or was I blindly building an ice house on a fiery furnace?

Three

Avoidance

Mark. Delete. Flush. Ignore. Breathe.

Four

Longing

Remembering your inner jokes and laughing alone in the bathroom. Cry, this is the point he washes your hair with so much attention, Kisses your neck, then lips. Gives his jacket to cover the consequence of your stubbornness.

Yearning for the memories shared.

Recall his sleepy face, bad dances, the fragrance of his cologne, and how he grips your waist. Cry.

Five

Redefining

Three months after, declare yourself single and not necessarily searching. Accept this cup and drink it slowly. Ignore the noise, let in air, every Tony will disgust you. Smirk at free smiles thrown way by cavaliers. Dress to kill, snap and post on Twitter, disregard his damage-control comments; hmmm Most Beautiful.

Six

Waiting

One year later, when your arid lips cannot remember how to kiss, take a sit near the window, watch the moon disappear into the cloud and hope It brings to you tomorrow love that is true.

USES OF A GUN

Point it at a woman
she will let you have your way
force her to keep the baby
ensure the baby returns
home from school lifeless
put everyone a bullet away
from death.

when a song punches your heart open, place a pillow over your face and let out a hysterical groan inwardly. become a mini museum under construction per annum with a semi-stuffed mini art gallery by the side to apologize for not being enough and still somehow give visitors stories to tell. tell a story of the sun unkissing rooftops and clouds disappearing into the sky unbothered. feel the desperation of a cock chasing a mother hen—this time not to publicly have sex but to angrily pick her feathers with its sharp beak and remind her how scared she should be of it. but the mother hen hides rage, turns it into love when she spreads inches of her wings to cover her chicks and dishes out her hurt to anything that tries to endanger her babes. stare at the image of your teacher that believes one man cannot rape a woman and souse in rage cooked in medium heat. sit in the pew watch the preacher make a young woman apologize to the church and god for being raped. play the tape in your head where you held the preacher by his scrotum and make his back a slate where god writes his apology for not keeping her from harm. everything you touch will turn to ashes from the moment you carry resentment that may not be yours but suits your collarbone. if you look again, you will recognize life to be an unnecessary requisite of things born and made. but shamefully, it fades to cries and uncertainty.

Unsolved Ecclesiastical Puzzle

Every day I pray that this white God forgives my black sins. Pats my back and says; girl, it's not your battle. Lucifer and I held this animosity too long that it fumes like fragile masculinity. Child, I want you to be everything I'm not. Feel the breast of a woman, lie, respond to the suffering world. Do not draw for verismo, just believe. Your brain will unravel quantum physics, and decipher rocket science but never question my certainty. I'm God—perfect in my judgment. I made black and white for variety and beauty, not hegemony. I toss the key to free-will but I instruct you to follow my route to my Shangri-la or drown in a lake of fire. I'm a man and a woman, I have a son to prove it. You can love whoever but don't forget to combat and slaughter each other.

SHE WEARS PINK

Hold the chronometer still
Let me hear her cry
come Home! my child
it took one breast

Let me see her smile
make a joke but this time
of having no breasts.
single lined cicatrices
standing side by side

Let me feel her silky hair
feed on the savory taste of her care
let me sing, MA, your baby is home
To help you bury parts of your body
that made me.

Breastless, happy, resilient
won all her battles—
to death she lost
gracefully.

IF GRIEF WAS WRITTEN IN CHAPTERS

Chapter 3

His mother's breast slipped out of his mouth Now, he can only
drink milk gotten from a cow
He eats beans when he wants cookies
His mama knows the best

Chapter 17

His first heartbreak has happened
hot air comes off his nostrils
his lungs are constricting
He is learning how to till the soil
Every door he opens
closes before he could enter

Chapter 75

There is a volcanic eruption in his heart
he saw his father get killed
he stood aloof and watched in terror
and confusion
Why is the world after his happiness?

Chapter 106

He is now a girl
lost her womb in an abortion process.
Every night in her dreams
a mountain of diapers swallows her
she dreams herself a boy
the first lips she kissed tasted like cherry
and later lemon

Chapter 220

Her husband smells like his secretary
Her stillness fuels the bond
there is a mighty Iroko tree in her heart
six children cutting it down with a penknife
Every day she buried herself in gold
and her tears washed her remains up

Chapter 388

She is now a table
her brother a chicken
it's Harmattan
and Christmas is here
The wood will make a fire
to keep them warm
they will have chicken for dinner
The first time they experienced happiness
was on the faces of their murders

Chapter 700

He is an old man without an heir
He feeds the world and clothes the poor
but no one was there to close his grave
Vultures feast on his remains
a generous man even in death

Chapter 888

On the flip side
An old woman
The witch
her eyes cause misfortune
A mother of rogues and prostitutes
Stoned and roasted for flies

Chapter one

The pain has no known address
grapples anything it can reach
it is without form
the end is not death.

EXPLAINING MY POLYCYSTIC OVARIAN SYNDROME TO MY MALE FRIEND HEARING IT FOR THE FIRST TIME

For beginners, to understand PCOS is to understand what it means to be a woman. Slim waist, flat tummy, hairless skin down to the butthole. A woman: a green garden that grins. An Illusion of beauty that transcends into a responsibility handed to every woman at birth. The world places its fantasies into your gate of self-worth, to make your existence a constant appeal for approval. To understand what it means to be a woman is to understand PCOS as a reversal of the expectations hanging on a woman's back. Her supposed lethal smile is now a cosplay costume. She grows scrotum-like endogens but not enough balls to face the mirror when her face looks like a raging wolf. She is not allowed to be imperfect—what is that hair doing on your face? When she wakes from her mood-induced sleep she finds out that she is now twice her original size. Summer body is not her forte, how will she explain a dark underarm, bumpy face in a perfect bikini on an imperfect body? She envies the smoothness of a beer bottle displayed on the shelf of a bar. She wakes up at midnight to pick strands and strands of hair off your jaw. It hurts but beauty is pain. She makes red patches on everything she touches, coats the spot with mud. It is ignoble to leak for weeks like a broken drainage pipe. When a boy across the street makes a joke about her hairy jaw, she laughs too. She thinks God had better jokes too, and excess testosterone to hand out to unsought donors. She wants to tell her mom that her period is 11 and half months late but she's not pregnant. She wonders if her bloom is over, who will pluck a non-flowering flower unlikely to sprout? Outside her door, a girl is walking amid five other girls playing this song in her head.

WHEN GIRL SAYS SHE LOVES YOU
—After Edwin Bodney's When a boy says he loves you.

She gives you her all. She has said that word several times and it tastes like pain, regret, lollygagging.

She knows you will be consistent with your inconsistency but she will ride with you.

When a girl says she loves you, she will cover you in her dreams, thoughts, and prayers. She will let you touch her holy.

She will tell you how she loves her tea and expects you to ask her how she loves her sex. 99.9% of your sex with her, she will fake weird noises to make you whole.

When a girl says she loves you, she doesn't want much. Just your time, care, and attention.

She can make honeycombs in her backyard but she will still want your sugar.

When a girl says she loves you, she knows the name and address of your secret lovers.

She comes to you damaged, with the scars of her prior encounters.

Every night she prays not to call you the name of the last people that worshiped her holy, wholly.

DUPLEX: BIG BIRDS NOW SING

Big birds now sing at night when hungry
        But sleep is how the demons go pronto

Demons go to sleep and wake a newborn
        Two legs in the mud, guilt is a flowing robe

Two muddy legs in a flowing robe of guilt
        On the east side, your mother's eyes are stars

On the east side, your mother's eyes are stars
        In broken pieces of hope, your eyes meet

Your eyes are made of broken pieces of hope
        In the country of your birth, you are a stranger

A stranger in the country of your birth
        Named in a language that hurts your tongue

In a language that hurts your tongue
        Your body is an item of the rancid laws

LIVING WITH ANXIETY

you set your alarm clock for 6 am but anxiety wakes up by 4:30, fills the room, and screams your name till you lose every iota of sleep. you check the time, it's 5 am. it makes you boil hot water for bath, to stop the coldness you feel in your stomach. reminds you, how much of a messy mess you are. anxiety climbs the podium to perform the poem you wrote last night, you, stuttering after asking numerous times not to share. it makes every eye a ball of fire reaching to burn you. it convinces you that people are cheering you for writing trash out of pity. anxiety is your friend but not the friendly type. anxiety makes you ignore the girl from the library you have been dying to talk to. anxiety embarrasses you and saves you from embarrassment.

anxiety follows you everywhere, sits with you in every room. plays in your head like your favourite song. anxiety sits you down when you ought to stand.

anxiety doesn't stop talking, you quit listening.

LET'S TALK ORGASM

A questionnaire goes around in a maternity ward asking four-time-moms the last time they had an orgasm. Some answered; during honeymoon, while others said; during university days. Then I wonder, the ways in which their babies were made. I wonder if marriage is a secret cult where women lose the right to their bodies, or another arid desert that produces wild fruits without water. A holy joke where Orgasm is barred. I wonder, why we teach women the Kamasutra, ways to please a man, without teaching her to love herself to climax. We fail to teach her that every part of her body is a temple worthy of worship. I wonder, if childbirth is a metaphor for a life sentence of awful coitus. She carries you, your babies, your home, but you fail to take her hands up to her 9th cloud, slowly, rapidly and intensely.

A DEEPER SLEEP

Sleep takes me to an unknown land
But I'm not a stranger to mystery
my mouth knows the sour taste of death
It makes dreams go stale
Purges hope and refills it with a flowing
stream of regret and grief

The hands; dry-ice-cold, replace plans
with heart-wrenching memories
Years of undying bonds in a box
headed for mother earth's belly

The first time you pass death
it wears a vague contortion
Ponder, what it
feels to be its eternal captive

PRAYING ME A RUDDY PARADISE

A rubicund Genie asked me to make three wishes for bringing her into existence again. I wished for my mother's children and her husband to be around for her 100th birthday anniversary. I wished for everything my family sold for survival to come back to us in 10 measures. I wished my poetry to taste sweet, savory, hot enough to be swallowed and cold enough to be held and admired, for it to leave a uniform aftertaste in the mouth of readers with a psychoactive agent that keeps the reader coming back to eat again. I could have wished for the combating planet to be at peace, the poor to be rich and the blind to open their eyes to see the colors this earth is made of, but I put myself first. I don't know what to do with grief if it drops on my leg unaware, or if I can wear it like the scars of an old soldier picked from numerous wars with stories to tell spectators. I choose abundance. I have tasted having enough and yet so little, how what your stomach calls is not what the mouth answers.

ENOUGH? THANKS GOODBYE.

Everything sprung from something.

Maybe they tap nutrients from the same manure,
like rage growing in the field of dislike.

The world becomes heavier when you try to carry
it's mass on a shoulder, reckless.

What are we?
A choir, an orchestra of things to be.

We are adding to the millions of chants
of frustration, abrasions and anguish.

For peace, we thirst
For freedom, we pray.

And love, we crave.

We aim not to build a never-seen castle
and chant in tongues unknown to man.

We try to add our songs to the medley, sung,
but we fear our voices will not echo out to be felt.

AND

STILLWATERS

ESCAPING THE DUNGEON

The best prison has no walls, It follows its captive around. The walls of every prison hold out opportunities, harvest-ready. On the day the door of a prison opens, the captive walks freely into another diagram of life. The second prison is dangerous when you swallow it carelessly, munching each morsel. It proceeds from the mouth of those that may love or not love you. The third prison is ferocious built with age-long materials like grief, anxiety, doubt, and self-sabotage into a monolith that can take any form. It wakes up before you, pours a cup of toiling blue and leaves your face, dreamy brown. Prisons are rent free abode, but in prison, you pay with tears and dashing hope.

Every time your mother says; go out and meet people, she means: get out of your head. Live. Just live.

CELESTIAL SHE

She is
a chunk of ember coated with ice
the rays in her smile
redeem lost souls
a healer_ she is
every heart she crosses
she leaves a big footprint
flaps her wings to provide a mild air
to show them what an
encounter with an angel feels like
a soul-mender_ she is
her light outshines her flaws
if she slips and falls
you will see her soar loftier.

A PRAYER ANSWERED

Every time the clock strikes eight, I search for greatness in my roots. I wonder if there is a plant in this land to be reaped. What will the farms yield? Will these maimed birds fly? When evenings come, the cold breeze from the Oji tree sweeps in hope. And reminds me of how my ancestors prayed for these days. How my tongue speaks of the melody of their Oja and Igba. How I never ceased to eat my words with ripe ilu. Every day I pray to be worthy of their dreams I carry, stick out my tongue to taste life and grab with my right a canvas and the other a brush, to paint the view I desire, and accept that I'm the answer to the prayers of my ancestors. That I learn the simple lessons from the Udara they left me; that life is an enmesh of sweet and sour, and could be sticky and messy. To learn to grow my faith like Udara seed and watch it bloom like the Udara tree and be that shade hankered for at the center.

MOON SISTERS

From grandma's Rafia waived kitchen
the moon watches above
in enthusiasm
reflecting the moon sisters
two cloud images at the heart
of the full moon
replicating my bustles.

IF MY HEAD IS MADE OF A FLOWING SEA

If my head is made of a flowing sea, storms will strike every five seconds. Plowing an engine that works for and against me, is a subtle hassle unexplained. Some days, I am a house built on aches waiting for a seism. On other days, I am a small wood cabin in a small Chinatown. Dreams come like a speeding vehicle on a bumpy road with airbags in the trunk. Rough. Capricious. If hope fuels a soul, what do I call the days I have no fuel? When will this head, wear a crown? Will basil seed sprout in this musty garden? If hope leaps, I will give fate a rightful chance to meander in a snowy city of lanky angels and beg Harmattan to leave the lips that kissed me goodbye, warm.

IF YOU ARE LOOKING FOR A WAR SONG, HERE IS ONE

my mind is seven graves deep

i feel one dendrite reaching for the next

my heart, the drum of two tribes in my head

when my legs melt to fear

i trust my hands to crawl me out of danger.

i learned survival before i learned my name.

sorry i'm making this poem about me.

let's talk about you.

your weary body houses a giant mind

the days you go to the shower to wash yourself with your tears.
the night you went to bed feeding on hope, work, and prayers.

i see you.

the days it rains only in your house and you come out drenched,
to the world you can't dry your dress. i see you.

the hours you spent stitching up your shattered heart and wore
it as an armour.

i see you.

the days you fake conversations with memories of mama to
spare a smile.

the days you had one candle but cut for a brother lest darkness
swallow him.

i see you.

the days you ask the wind blow you to a land of no green.

i see you.

mars, jupiter and saturn are returning your crown pluto disappeared with.

this is not a promise of a road smooth and tiled, bumps are ahead with grapes at every bend.

i see you, the universe sees you.

LOVING MYSELF BLUE

Have you seen beauty fade?
My beauty turned into food
can feed seven nations fat.
Deep. Kalon!
My hands are made of ceaseless potential
My hips wiggle without Jigida
I speak hope and make mountains bow
The earth moves to the beat of my heart
I am nature's true pride
Built like an ancient river goddess,
a masterpiece in progress
Wait, I'm no braggadocio—
this is the song I sing for myself on slow
and gloomy days
You hear me say I'm beautiful, but I mean
I abhor my never to be flattened stomach
and I wish to be seven inches taller
I say I love myself and my mind is at peace,
but I mean, am I worthy of love?
Will these nightmares ever stop?
Will my ancestors in the belly of the creek
of Georgia smile when they hear you call me Georgia?

AFRICAN GIRL

An African girl__
The seed of an ebony goddess
The dream of this black empress
The hope of the coming Nubian queen
Bleaching out my originality
to feign perfection like it exists
Ashamed of the body I did not create
Picking up an accent that ridicules my mother tongue—
eating my dialect like it's sour
Required from; a smile to help stiffen balls
of men with zero sense of humor
Shaping myself to fit the societal definition of beauty—
but if beauty has a standard it should be me
Expected to be smart and dumb when needed
like a mixture of water and oil
They teach me to be too humble so they can override me
then I become too apologetic and lose my confidence
They want me to be rich but not too rich,
to keep their ego bloated
Yes, they want a hyena in a chicken's body
So hear me this African girl
Be you, letting all of your light out,
dish out your fiercest look—
adorn yourself with goals, and big dreams
Never stop becoming
You are nature's most precious art
An African girl.

REBIRTH OF THE DANCING SUN

On a slow and sunny morning
the hour of the dancing sun
the glory of mother nature vibes
to the cheer for our fatherland.

On a gusty and listless noon
the hour of the dancing sun
the earth wails in despair
whispering the tale of its journey
to my tepid ears; the cry of
an heir-less kingdom waiting in sacrifice
and a strand of hope.

On a sluggish and arduous night
The dancing sun collides with the moon.
the night becomes hasty
turning the cry for a deceased KING
into the cry of a newborn PRINCE.

DREAM AND DESIRE

When I grow up, I want to be the key that unlocks mirth. Fill the universe with glee.

Drown depression in the ocean of possibilities, chew anxiety, and crush its bones to dust. Let whoever be whatever, plant empathy in every heart. Till the field with people's excuses and let forgiveness grow.

When I grow up, I desire life to taste of old wine. Of grief; a metaphor for hope. Peace becomes more than imagery so love can touch those that hanker for it.

NOT TODAY!

The dog barks, It's 2 am
but your eyelids are standing
miles apart.
You are donning a dreamy body
on a heavy mind.
Eerie images of known ghosts
flashing on your window pane
The room smells of anxiety,
your shaky legs cannot carry you.
Turn down the volume of
the skirmish in your head
Wrap your fears up with a duvet
pull your eyelids closer to each other.

MAYBE MY WATER BROKE AGAIN IN MY SLEEP

When a poem does not have hands a poet cuts pieces of her flesh to give it limbs and wings as long as she's the only one bleeding the world may never know her hurt. A mug does not say what it carries but it envies the wine glass for being honest and will not hear it say cover me and keep this alcoholic sober for one more day. When the head starts to mock the legs for being slow it asks it what it means to be carried by the neck. Only a pot knows how it convinces the fish to dress differently in water and oil. A bachelor laughing at a married man's woes forgets how cold reaches for his soul at midnight. In today's news, an amputee explains death better than the dead. A barren woman sits and prays for the sun to go down into her stomach and lend her what to bear at dawn. A poem picks up misery as a relic and places it in the hand of the reader, formless. Still, many afflictions lie unattended. The first time you dream of your parent's death, the children of an evil woman sets up fire camps in your stomach. When you wake you slowly drop your heart on the shelf, you are still a poet and this is not your first nightmare. In your first nightmare, you died of love, warmth, and laughter.

WHAT THE LORD HATH MADE

—After Ebony Stewart's poem, Eve.

I know some days, you wear your body like another sick apology.
You pin opinions about your body like a tag on your chest. You
look in the mirror and you don't feel beautiful. You send a smile
to atone for your scars before you arrive. To you, life is a
runaway, and you're not a supermodel in yesterday's magazine.
But today, you will enter every room and your body will
announce: *HEY, LOOK WHAT THE LORD HATH MADE.*

OXYTOCIN INFLUX REVERSAL

If you catch what was never thrown at you but fits your open
palms,

you will desire to be touched in places your mother will not
approve.

Get behind your keyboard, hide your heart exploding within,

with every strand of dopamine galloping through your brain.

Pump your doubt into mental blockades till your walls are out
of reach.

When your phone rings again,

try not to suppress your breath channel.

If you attempt to cry about something that left

remember it was barely there.

Child, hold unto what wants to be held.

FATE MEETS FAITH

Have faith on rainy days
Wait for glory days
Pain will slowly fade
Gains surely made
Swerve and cross the bar
Keep going, the road's still far
You have mother's heart
Wear your father's hat
Approach the throne
And accept your crown.

AGAINST THE CURRENT

When you find yourself drowning
don't worry about the bags you carry
glide your hands softly in the water
allow the world to carry itself
Try not to breathe underwater
raise your head and inhale strength
the fear of facing death
will loosen the knots of your legs
stand
call loudly your mother's name
her heart will guide you
pray to your father's ghost
when the water pushes your back
cling to the weight of your ancestors
they will hold you firm
offer a sacrifice of hearty songs
to the sea goddess
ask her to spare you this day
The ocean will throw you up
open your mouth and let out
every anxiety you gulped in
breathe
For the rest of your life
pretend you are made of salt

AMARANTHINE AS WORTHY SYNONYM FOR POETS

Often times I wonder what I will be when these words that I conceive as it builds me, finish. What I will do if I become an old bag of bad vocabularies that cannot stand each other. A dictionary washed off its essence by the rain sitting in a roadside dumpster. Will I chatter down the surging youngsters trying to figure out what these words want with them, to cover the depth of my emptiness or hold the bar up enough for the up and coming to infiltrate? I have searched for a reason to hold unto this pen. There's a dead lizard with a league of ants carrying away morsels of its remains. A poem is in everything. Feed the world even when your heart retires from pumping.

READY OR NOT

When life hands you
a box full of nothingness
Don't cry
Keep it dry

Burn it to ashes
paint with it on the left
side of your face
like a soldier; battle ready
FIGHT.

You made it to the end.

Thank you.